The Days that Changed the
WORLD

Mark Wright

Badger Publishing Limited
Oldmedow Road,
Hardwick Industrial Estate,
King's Lynn PE30 4JJ
Telephone: 01438 791037

www.badgerlearning.co.uk

2 4 6 8 10 9 7 5 3

The Days that Changed the World ISBN 978-1-78464-038-5

Publisher: Susan Ross
Senior Editor: Danny Pearson
Publishing Assistant: Claire Morgan
Designer: Fiona Grant
Series Consultant: Dee Reid

Photos: Cover image: REX
Page 5: © Visions of America, LLC/Alamy
Page 6: © ClassicStock/Alamy
Page 7: © Michael Flippo/Alamy
Page 9: © Deco/Alamy
Page 11: © MARKA/Alamy
Page 13: © The Print Collector/Alamy
Page 15: Universal History Archive/Un/REX
Page 16: © Philip Pound/Alamy
Page 17: © David Osborn/Alamy
Page 19: Daily Mail/REX
Page 20: © age fotostock Spain, S.L./Alamy
Page 21: © Roger Bamber/Alamy
Page 22: REX
Page 23: NASA images
Page 24: NASA images
Page 25: NASA images
Page 27: © Pictorial Press Ltd/Alamy
Page 28: © AF archive/Alamy
Page 29: © Prisma Illustration/iStock
Page 30: © PSL Images/Alamy

Attempts to contact all copyright holders have been made.
If any omitted would care to contact Badger Learning, we will be happy to make appropriate arrangements.

The Days that Changed the WORLD

Contents

Badger

Vocabulary

aeroplane	declaration
astronaut	prequel
broadcast	pursuit
coronation	Sea of Tranquility

I. The American Declaration of Independence

When:

4 July 1776

Where:

Philadelphia, USA

What happened?

America was already angry that it was ruled by Britain.
Then the British Parliament raised the taxes that
the Americans had to pay.

The Americans decided to fight for their freedom.

That war was called the American Revolutionary War and it started in 1775.

On 4th July 1776, one of the leaders of the revolution, Thomas Jefferson, wrote the American Declaration of Independence.

How it changed the world:

The document said that America was now separate from British rule and would become a new nation – the United States of America.

It said that 'all men are created equal' and that everyone has the right to 'life, liberty and the pursuit of happiness'.

Some people say the Declaration of Independence was the most important document ever written.

It inspired other people around the world to fight for their rights.

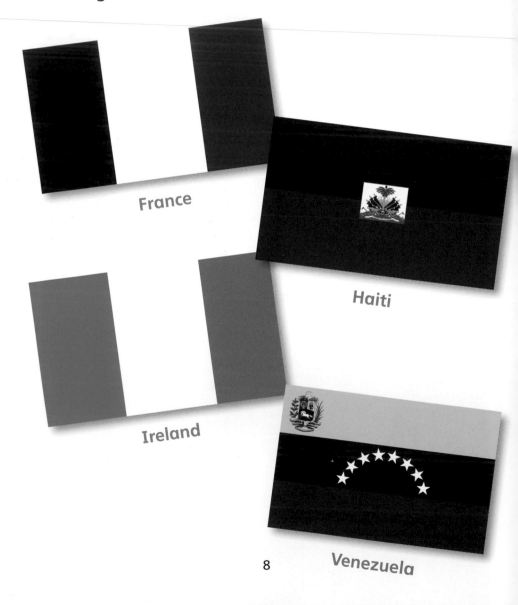

France

Haiti

Ireland

Venezuela

8

It also marked the birth of the United States of America, which would become the biggest superpower in the world.

WOW! facts

Independence Day is celebrated every year on 4th July in the USA. It is a public holiday – and there are lots of fireworks!

2. The death of Queen Victoria

When:

22 January 1901

Where:

Osborne House, Isle of Wight

What happened?

After 63 years, seven months and two days on the throne of Great Britain, Queen Victoria died at the age of 81.

How it changed the world:

Victoria was queen longer than any other British king or queen.

While she was on the throne, Britain had become the most powerful nation in the world.

Queen Victoria's son, Edward, became King after his mother died. He was Edward VII but he was always called Bertie.

Edward VII was 60 when he came to the throne and he was king for only nine years.

When Victoria was queen everything was very prim and proper. It was even thought rude to say the word 'leg' so people said 'limb' instead.

Women were frowned upon if they were seen on bicycles and they had to sit side-saddle when riding a horse.

Times were changing by the time Edward came to the throne. He liked drinking, shooting and having fun with his friends. He was a lively and likable king.

Although neither Victoria nor Edward were responsible for any of the changes, their reigns came to represent two very different eras in British history.

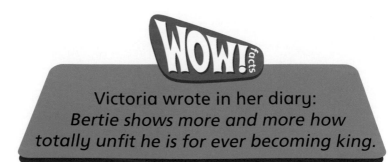

WOW! facts

Victoria wrote in her diary:
Bertie shows more and more how totally unfit he is for ever becoming king.

At the start of the 20th Century the world was changing and Britain began to lose its power. After the death of Queen Victoria, Britain was never the same again.

3. The first powered aeroplane flight

When:

17 December 1903

Where:

Kitty Hawk, North Carolina, USA

What happened?:

Brothers Orville and Wilbur Wright built the first aircraft that could actually fly. Lots of people had been trying to build an aircraft but the planes never took off.

How it changed the world:

The first flight made by the Wright brothers lasted just 12 seconds and was only over a distance of 120 feet, but it was the start of flying history.

After the Wright brothers' success, aeroplanes quickly became better and better, and less than 20 years later, planes were speeding across the skies.

WILBUR WRIGHT

Before aeroplanes were invented, people had to travel by steam train or steam ship.

It took 60 days to travel by sea to Australia. Now you can fly there in one day!

Only one of the Wright brothers could fly in their plane at a time.

Now the largest jets can take 525 passengers and 22 crew, two captains and two flight officers.

WOW! facts

Guess what Orville and Wilbur Wright called their plane? The Flyer!

4. The invention of the television

When:

2 October 1925

Where:

London

What happened?

A Scottish inventor called John Logie Baird was the first person to show TV pictures to the world.

John Logie Baird was not the only inventor working on creating a television but his invention was very important.

In 1924, Baird used boxes, biscuit tins, sewing needles, card and the motor from an electric fan to make his first TV.

His first TV picture showed a cross cut out of card.

In 1925, Baird made better TV pictures. The first person to appear on television was Baird's office boy, who was called William.

How it changed the world:
The fuzzy black and white pictures made by Baird soon developed into the most popular form of mass entertainment ever.

TV programmes attracted huge audiences, for example, the coronation of Queen Elizabeth II in 1953 and the Apollo moon landing in 1969.

WOW! facts

The highest rated television broadcast in the United Kingdom was the 1966 World Cup Final with a combined audience of 32.3 million.

5. The first moon landing

When:

20 July 1969

Where:

The moon

What happened?

Astronaut Neil Armstrong became the first person to walk on the moon after the Apollo 11 lunar module touched down in the Sea of Tranquility.

How it changed the world:

In 1961, the American president John F Kennedy had promised that America would put a man on the moon by 1969.

The Russians also wanted to be the first country to send a man to the moon, so the race was on!

The Americans won the race!

As Neil Armstrong stepped down from the lunar module he said:

"That's one small step for a man; one giant leap for mankind."

These words are possibly the most famous words ever spoken.

Armstrong and another astronaut called Buzz Aldrin were on the moon for two and a half hours.

They planted an American flag and collected moon rock. But the most important thing about the moon landing was that it proved it was possible.

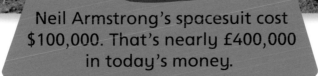

WOW! facts

Neil Armstrong's spacesuit cost $100,000. That's nearly £400,000 in today's money.

6. Star Wars is released at the cinema

When:

25 May 1977

Where:

Los Angeles, USA

What happened?

Star Wars, written and directed by George Lucas, and starring Mark Hamill, Harrison Ford and Carrie Fisher, opened in cinemas.

How it changed the world:

The film's state-of-the-art effects created a new industry for special effects in Hollywood.

It was also the first film to make a lot of money from spin-off action figures and it made Harrison Ford into one of the biggest movie stars in the world.

Darth Vader's famous voice was made by putting a microphone inside a scuba mask and then recording it.

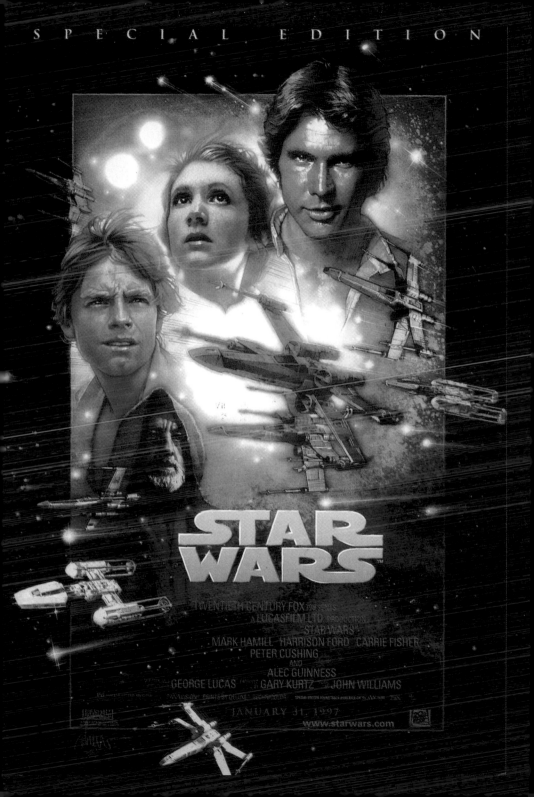

There were two sequels to the first *Star Wars* film: *The Empire Strikes Back* (1980) and *Return of the Jedi* (1983).

Sixteen years after the release of the trilogy's final film, the first in a new prequel trilogy of films was released.

Star Wars started the tradition of blockbuster movie trilogies.

Without *Star Wars*, there would be no *Lord of the Rings* movies, *Harry Potter* or *The Hunger Games* – and no new *Star Wars* films to look forward to!

7. The launch of Facebook

When:

4 February 2004

Where:

Harvard University, USA

What happened?

Harvard student, Mark Zuckerberg, launched a website as a way to connect university students.

How it changed the world:

Facebook became a new way of sharing information across the world.

By 2014, Facebook had 1.23 billion active users.

Questions

Who wrote the American Declaration of Independence? *(page 6)*

When did Queen Victoria die? *(page 10)*

What did Orville and Wilbur Wright call their plane? *(page 17)*

What things did John Logie Baird use to make his first TV? *(page 19)*

What famous words did Neil Armstrong say when he first stepped onto the moon? *(page 24)*

When was Facebook launched? *(page 29)*

Index